Gasoline Secrets

Dave Nassaney

David Nassaney Visit our website at:

www.GasolineSecrets.com
www.GasolineExpert.com

Printed in the United States of America.

Secon Printing:
June, 2022 ISBN: 978-0-9849831-4-8

A big thank you goes to God for His miraculous provision in providing me with a great gas station. I might add that He did this during the gas shortage of 1979 when gas stations were simply not available at any affordable price.

Table of Contents

Foreword

The title of this book, "Gasoline Secrets" Comes from the fifty-years that I have been in the gas station business, owning six at one point, and now have downsized to just one in Castaic Lake, CA. My late dad, Joe Nassaney, was also in the business since 1945, when he opened his first gas station in the Bronx, NY.

It is my hope that this book will reveal to you that the gas station dealer is not making millions of dollars off the consumer through higher and higher gas prices. Most gas station owners are just small businessmen and businesswomen struggling to survive. Most national franchisors, like McDonalds, have as their number one goal to help their franchisees become successful. However, based on the oil company's business practices with their franchisees, it would appear that they often go out of their way to insure the dealer's failure and ultimate demise. I will provide many examples in the following chapters of how the oil company's business dealings tremendously hurt the dealer's chances of survival.

In the past, some observers have speculated that the oil companies were treating the gas station dealers unfairly in order to take over their franchise operations so they could turn them into direct-run company operations. But today that argument does not seem plausible, given the fact that the oil companies have been selling their gas station assets to get out of the retail side of their business. Instead, they now prefer concentrating on oil exploration and gasoline refining operations, which are much more lucrative than collecting rents as a landlord and maintaining the equipment at their stations. The big oil companies also don't want the headaches of actually running their company-operated properties any more.

These headaches include constantly making costly environmental upgrades to their sites, paying hefty fines when not in compliance with the ever-changing rules, and having to deal with all of the problems associated with employing gas station personnel. After all, if the dealer goes broke trying to survive all of the burdens put on them by their suppliers, then the oil company can simply sell the unsuccessful dealer's location to a larger wholesaler. That wholesaler may operate hundreds of locations more successfully than a dealer can because of their lower overhead. The oil companies would still have many options available to them in their quest to manipulate that wholesaler's prices and to control the supply of fuel. I will discuss these tactics used in the following chapters.

I have been the owner of six gas stations in California since 1976. Before that, I had worked at or managed numerous gas stations for several different family members since 1966. Prior to that, my father had owned, worked at or managed gas stations and garages since 1945 in New York City and in California. We have seen many changes in the gas station business over the years.

This book is purely for your entertainment and knowledge. I discovered a long time ago that no matter where I went in social gatherings, the conversation would eventually come around to me and what I did for a living. To my amazement, I would often find myself sharing experiences from work to a growing number of very interested listeners. The crowd of people hanging on to my every word at these group get-togethers would grow, since it was rare that anyone actually knew a gas station owner. I later find out from my friends that I and my gas station stories were often the life of the party. I quickly developed a routine for telling the most popular and outrageous of these experiences, and I have been told that they were always entertaining.

There was never a shortage of questions that people would ask me concerning my station and the oil companies. Perhaps you have some gas station questions of your own that may get answered in this book. Questions like: "What is it really like dealing with those big oil companies? Do you get to set your own gas prices or do the oil companies dictate which prices to charge us? Why does the price of gas go up so quickly and so often? Is all gasoline the same or are some brands better than others? Is premium really better for my car and worth the extra cost?"

Big oil companies are probably the most distrusted and hated of entities out there. Along with attorneys, banks and insurance companies they lack the public's trust and respect. Most oil companies have more assets and gross profit than many third world countries do. Read on and I will try to answer all of the above questions. I will also share some funny, entertaining, sad, shocking, and interesting details about my particular gas station experiences during the last forty-five years. I don't think that anyone really knows the truth about oil company practices, but hopefully you will gain a better perspective from someone who was just a little bit closer to it all than most people were. Along with you, I too was getting ripped off by the oil companies through excessively high rents, zone pricing, forcing us to buy truckloads of oil, pressuring us to lower our prices to sell more fuel at less profit, etc.

CHAPTER 1

Forty-Six Years in the Gas Business

My gas station career started when I was only twelve years old at my dad's Burbank gas station. I was expected to work there after school and on weekends, so I quickly learned the work ethic that I saw my dad exhibit daily. He was a very good mechanic who was also very charming and likeable to his customers.

Being a mechanic is very similar to being a doctor. A patient/doctor relationship is a very special bond that is not easily broken, especially when you find a knowledgeable and experienced Medical Doctor (M.D.) that you like and have a good bedside manner with. So, it is also with a customer and his car. A car is a very complicated piece of machinery that requires a knowledgeable and experienced "Doctor of Motors" (D.M.) that you must like and trust. This person should be fair with their prices and honest with their diagnosis of the patient's car. This was my dad. He had a reputation for being charismatic and had a very loyal following. In fact, in the rare event that he would move his business to another location, his customers would often track him down and drive several hours to bring their cars to him for repairs. The oil company executives also loved

him. They would offer him any available station that he wanted because they knew that he could transform even the most unprofitable location into a lucrative money maker for the oil company and for himself.

He would also work on the priests' and nuns' cars for free as a service to the Catholic Church and school where I attended just down the block from his gas station. I think he may have believed that his services would insure him a spot in heaven (and might even contribute to better grades for myself). If nothing else, I'm sure that he hoped his generosity to the church would tilt the scales of spiritual justice a little in his favor. He was so well liked in his town that there was even some talk of him running for Mayor at one time. He was also very popular and well respected with the Burbank city officials and rotary clubs who also brought their cars to him to be fixed. He was even endorsed by his peers to run for the coveted position of "Grand Exalted Ruler" at the local Elks Lodge in Burbank; however, he just didn't have the time to campaign or devote to the post.

My dad taught me the business well, and I learned firsthand from him how to treat our customers. As I became a more proficient mechanic, I began to develop my own loyal following. I remember one mistake I made on my first day on the job. I changed the oil in a car and saw a puddle of oil as I backed it off of the garage hoist. I suddenly remembered that I forgot to put the drain plug back in the crankcase. Fortunately, my dad was there watching and later explained to me that I had to have a mental checklist of every step of the repair or service so that something like that would never happen again. It could have cost me a new engine and so I made sure that it never happened again.

Back in the 1970's, it seemed like there were three or four gas stations on every corner. There was also a shortage of dealers to run those gas stations. The oil companies used to pay us a one-hundred-dollar incentive for finding them a dealer who qualified. The qualification for a new dealer was that he had to be breathing (their standards were very low back then).

We came from a very big Middle Eastern family in Brooklyn. In 1960, my dad was the first one in the family to leave the cold of New York

City (and his gas station in the Bronx) to move to sunny Burbank, California. One by one, our family members followed him to the west coast: cousins, nephews, uncles, in-laws (and out-laws.) My dad began to recommend them to the oil company executives, with whom he had enjoyed a very good relationship. This enabled my family members to get their own gas stations. My dad would do this only after having them work at his gas station for about a year so that they could learn the trade under his watchful eye.

They wouldn't make much money during this training period; often just enough to pay their bills. Afterward, he would lend them the money that they needed to open their own gas stations. At one point we had a dozen or so locations run by various family members all over Burbank and Glendale.

I worked at each one when I was a teenager. I especially enjoyed working weekends at my cousin's station, which for some reason had a lot of really cute female patrons; it was a fun job. Fuel was very cheap in those days. Regular gas would often sell between 22 and 25 cents per gallon during a gas sale (or gas war as we called it). After a month or two when the gas war was over, the price would go back up to 35 cents per gallon overnight. This cycle was very predictable. Prices would then come down a penny at a time for a couple of months, and then go up overnight again when they got too low.

In those days, we would pump the customer's gas for them. Some of you might be too young to remember this, but at one time our free services included washing front and back windows with a squirt bottle and paper towels, not with the messy squeegees that are used today. We would always ask the customer if they wanted us to check their oil and water, and would often recommend oil changes when their oil looked dark. We checked battery terminals for corrosion, and popped in new air filters when they were too dirty. We would even check tires for air pressure and tread pattern. If there was any uneven tread wear, we would recommend a wheel alignment or a tire balance. It was easy to bring in extra income just by opening the hood of a car, since most people neglected their periodic maintenance. That neglect is even worse today because no one is actively checking and reminding people to do these services every time they get gas. In those days maps were free, there was no self-service, and you didn't have to pay before your gas was pumped.

After I married my wife and graduated college, I partnered with my dad in a failing gas station that we acquired from my brother. We immediately turned it around by building up the garage business using the methods described above. After three years, we outgrew that station and I was able to get one of my own in a small community called Castaic Lake. My dad ended up getting one in Northridge

CHAPTER 2

The First Gas Shortage, 1973

In 1973 (when I wasn't studying or attending to classes at U.S.C.) I would often be working at one of my relatives' gas stations. I was allowed to get free gas at my dad's station in Van Nuys, California. Then one day when I drove into his gas station to fill up, I discovered that I couldn't get close enough to the pumps because of the long line of cars waiting to get gas. I was not in the habit of listening to the news back then, so I really didn't know anything about the gas shortage or most of the events that led up to it until I actually saw the lines at my dad's station.

Being the owner's son, I felt that I had the right to simply pull in front of a car that was in line at the pumps and attempt to squeeze into a very tight spot to use an available dispenser. This   time, however, I was immediately confronted by angry motorist who demanded to know why I had cut into the line in front of his car. I had to think quickly, so I spotted my gas station uniform shirt in the back seat of my car and immediately put it on. I then told the individual who had confronted me that I worked there and had to fill up my car before I could begin my shift. He then politely backed off and apologized. The last thing any motorist wanted to do during a gas shortage was to upset a gas station employee.

Back then, I would love to go and eat at restaurants while wearing my uniform. I was always the most popular person there. People would often strike up conversations with me and inquire about where I worked. They would also usually ask if there was any way that I could sell them some gasoline before we opened to avoid the long lines. It felt nice to suddenly be so popular; I enjoyed the notoriety.

Many of my dad's faithful repair customers would be given special appointments in which they could buy their gas from him before he would open to the general public. They were very grateful that they didn't have to wait in the long lines like the others did. Before laws were passed by some states prohibiting discrimination of gasoline sold by dealers, many stations would put up signs that read, "Regular Customers Only." In essence, if the workers at those stations didn't recognize them as a regular customer, they couldn't buy any gas from that station. Instead, those customers were told to go buy their gas from where they ordinarily went before the shortage. The logic was that the station only had so much gas allotted to them to sell in a day, and so they wanted to sell it only to their loyal customers.

Before the gas shortage, motorists who were not faithful to one gas station (shopping around town looking for the lowest price) would often waste more gasoline looking for that low price than they would have saved by just purchasing their gas from one location. As a result, these customers often found themselves having to wait in long gas lines because they were not invited by the dealer to purchase their gas before the station opened up for business. In a way, these customers were being paid back for their disloyalty. Friends, relatives and faithful customers would always get their gas by special appointment before the station opened up to the public. It felt good to reward our loyal customers that way, and they never forgot that courtesy that we extended to them when things eventually returned back to normal.

For those of you who are unfamiliar with how the first energy crisis of 1973 came about, let me give you a brief history lesson. Some of you may not have even been born by 1973 and are unaware of what I am about to describe. The first oil crisis started in October 1973.

The members of the Organization of Arab Petroleum Exporting Countries (OAPEC), which consists of the Arab members plus Egypt, Syria and Tunisia, proclaimed an oil embargo. This was in response to the U.S. decision to re-supply the Israeli military during the Yom Kippur war. It lasted until March 1974.

The situation became critical because of the Mideast War. Arab nations announced a monthly reduction by 5% of the petroleum they would ship to countries known to be friendly with Israel.

President Nixon stated, "Because of the war, most of the Middle Eastern oil producers have reduced overall production and cut off their shipments of oil to the United States. By the end of the month, more than two million barrels a day of oil expected to be imported into the United States will no longer be available." He went on to say, "We must therefore face up to a very stark fact: we are heading toward the most acute shortage of energy since World War II. Our supply of petroleum this winter will be at least 10% short of our anticipated demands, and it could fall short by as much as 17%. Because of the energy crisis, the lights on the national Christmas tree would not be lit as a symbolic gesture."

While driving was not banned in the United States, the President did request highway speeds be lowered. Nixon went on to say, "Consistent with safety and economic considerations, I am also asking Governors to take steps to reduce highway speed limits to 50 miles per hour. If adopted on a nationwide basis, this action alone could save over two- hundred thousand barrels of oil a day just by reducing the speed limit to 50 miles per hour."

Nixon continued, "To be sure that there is enough oil to go around for the entire winter all over the country, it will be essential for all of us to live and work in lower temperatures. We must ask everyone to lower the thermostat in your home by at least six degrees so that we can achieve a national daytime average of sixty-eight degrees. Incidentally, my doctor tells me that in a temperature of sixty-six to sixty-eight degrees, you're really healthier than when it's seventy-five to seventy-eight, if that's any comfort."

No one really knew how long things would continue to be difficult. It was a shock for people to realize how dependent we were on foreign Middle-East oil. For the first time ever, laws were passed to prohibit us from putting up Christmas lights, to not drive faster than 50 MPH, to close all gas stations on Sundays, to turn down our thermostats, for companies to trim their work hours and to turn off any unnecessary lights at businesses and homes after dark. Even the Las Vegas strip went dark. In fact, in some countries like the Netherlands, driving was banned completely on Sundays.

Congress even voted that the country return to Daylight Savings Time during the winter months. This made parents very uneasy sending their young children out to wait for the school bus while it was still dark outside. In California, laws were passed making motorists purchase their fuel only on odd calendar days if their license plate ended with an odd number, and only on even calendar days for plates ending with even numbers.

As oil supplies contracted because of the embargo, the United States held prices artificially low. Government officials, fearing a return of the previous year's frigid winter in the Northeast, then ordered refineries to produce an oversupply of heating oil instead of meeting the demand for gasoline. This only made the shortage worse.

Many major energy policies have changed as a result of the energy crisis of 1973, including the elimination of oil price controls, the establishment of the Energy Department as a cabinet-level agency and the establishment of the Strategic Petroleum Reserve, which now contains about 563 million barrels in underground caverns in Louisiana.

According to Henry Linden, a professor at the Illinois Institute of

Technology, the reserve is designed to supply the nation - which consumes about nineteen million barrels a day - until any future oil crisis has passed. It gives the U.S. a safety valve in the event of another embargo. War or terrorism could still reduce the world oil supply temporarily, but other suppliers would increase exports to fill the breach, prices would temporarily rise, dampening demand, and the U.S. could tap its strategic reserve to stabilize prices.

The U.S. also approved the construction of a major Trans-Alaskan pipeline. The pipeline was built between 1974 and 1977 after the 1973 oil crisis caused a sharp rise in oil prices in the United States. This rise made exploration of the Prudhoe Bay oil field economically feasible. Environmental, legal, and political debates followed the discovery of oil at Prudhoe Bay in 1968, and the pipeline was built only after the oil crisis provoked the passage of legislation designed to remove legal and environmental challenges to the project.

When things finally returned to normal in March, 1974, it didn't take long for most Americans and regulators to forget all about conserving energy. After a couple years or so, American's short memories allowed them to slowly go back to their old habits of wasting energy once again. Speed limits increased, thermostats went up, and sales of larger more comfortable gas guzzler cars increased while demand for more fuel-efficient smaller imports waned. But then it happened all over again in 1979 for different reasons, and all of our conservation memories returned.

Suspicions of oil company greed again surfaced because of the huge windfall profits that the shortages added to their balance sheets. Congress even enacted a windfall profits tax so that the oil companies wouldn't unfairly profit from the shortage. Never before had an industry been singled out and taxed at a higher rate just because Congress deemed that their profits were excessive.

CHAPTER 3
The Second Gas Shortage, 1979

It was June of 1979 when I took over the gas station in Castaic, California. At that time, we were going through the second gas shortage, which occurred because the Shah of Iran was being deposed as a result of a revolution and civil war in his country. A group of Islamic students and militants even took over the American Embassy in Tehran and held hostages in support of the Iranian Revolution.

The United States decided to boycott Iranian oil because Iran's new leader, the Ayatollah Khomeini, supported the student's actions. Sixty-six Americans were held hostage for 444 days. President Jimmy Carter called the hostages "victims of terrorism and anarchy", adding that the "United States will not yield to blackmail". Americans were also outraged that the doctrine of diplomatic immunity was totally ignored.

As a result of the boycott, the oil companies allocated only a percentage of a station's gasoline purchase history to that dealer. I was only given 36,000 gallons of gas, instead of the normal 70,000 gallons, that I could have very easily sold that first month that I opened. In order to keep selling fuel every day, I had to ration my gasoline sold by allowing customers to purchase only ten gallons at a time. We only stayed open 5 hours a day to accomplish this and we also closed on Sundays, our busiest day. Odd/even rationing was also being observed, matching odd/even calendar days to the motorist's license plate number.

To make matters worse, the South Coast Air Quality Management District (SCAQMD), the governmental agency that enforces air quality regulations in Southern California, just happened to simultaneously implement the long-awaited vapor recovery nozzle. The combination of long gas lines and the confusing bulky gas nozzle with a rubber boot was a very frustrating experience for us and for our customers. The nozzle would only work when it was fully depressed into the fill neck of the car. Customers did not know how to operate it. Instructions on the pump were often ignored or not even seen. We repeatedly had to provide the customer with full service by pumping their gas for them because they didn't know how to correctly use the new nozzles.

It was a disturbing time. Long lines of cars wrapped around streets adjacent to gas stations for as far as a mile in most cases.

It was almost impossible for us to stop selling gas so that we could shut down for the day. People were so desperate that they would drive up and down the streets looking for an open gas station. When they would finally find one, a mad dash to the pumps would ensue. These frantic gas customers were capable of anything. I heard on the news that one very tired and frustrated gas station attendant had a gas nozzle in one hand and a cigarette lighter in the other hand and threatened to squirt and set on fire an irate customer if he didn't back off.

When it was finally time to shut down our gas pumps to close, tempers would often flare. We attempted to tell the last customer in line that we had sold our allocation for the day and couldn't sell any more gas or else we would run out for the month. You can only imagine how these customers felt after waiting in line for nearly three hours, finally arriving onto the property only to be told that they couldn't have any gas. It was very stressful and heartbreaking for both of us.

It was especially very problematic trying to fill up my own car. I usually tried to do it when the station had orange traffic cones all around the pumps so it looked like we were closed. However, anyone driving around looking for an open gas station would instantly spot a car at the pumps and immediately pull in and expect to get gas as well.

We finally came up with a system to start closing down two hours early by putting a big orange traffic cone on top of the last car in line. That car was usually about a mile down the road. If it was a Chevy, for example, I would visit the line again in about an hour to see how close that Chevy was to the pumps. But for some reason, the line looked just as long as it did an hour ago. I then noticed that my orange cone was now on a Ford, twenty-three cars behind the Chevy. This was just some of the craziness that we all had to deal with trying to close down for the day.

Another time, a man in line refused to pay for his gas. He said that he paid some guy in a gas station uniform that was collecting money in advance from waiting motorists. The only problem was that he didn't work for us. He was just a very creative opportunistic thief who got away with several people's hard- earned cash. Gas thievery was also rampant. People would go to bed after filling up their cars only to wake up the next morning to find an empty gas tank that someone had siphoned during the night. Locking gas caps became very popular. Even gas stations had to lock their underground storage tanks because they were sometimes robbed during the night by thieves with a hand pump.

As I stated earlier, our gas station was at a lake resort location right off the busiest Interstate in the country, and maybe even the world. Interstate 5 actually connects three countries; Canada, the U.S. and Mexico. It also connects three states; Washington, Oregon and California in a non-stop, center-divided freeway (no traffic signals, intersections, or stop signs). Furthermore, the last stop for gas services before reaching our station was twenty-seven miles north of us on a very steep non-populated grade called the Grapevine. It got its name not because of the old two-lane road that would wind back and forth resembling a grapevine, but for the canyon it passed through with its wild grapes that still grow along the original road.

This grade was infamous for its high accident rate before the road was straightened and widened. There are escape ramps branching off both sides of the downward part of the road for heavy trucks whose brakes fail on this very long 6% grade. The road is still occasionally closed due to heavy snowfall during winter storms. It also closes for brush fires during the summer season. As the Grapevine is the major route between Northern and Southern California, any closure is a major disruption to traffic along the West Coast.

Motorists typically came into our gas station with their gas gauges on empty, while their bladders were on full. They needed both fuel and a toilet very badly. Many would simply coast down the grade, having already run out of gas, and be stranded at the bottom of the hill. There were no hotels back then in Castaic so numerous stranded motorists (some with children) had to sleep in their cars until we reopened the next day. If it happened to be on a Saturday after our already reduced business hours, then they would be marooned there until Monday morning (since we closed on Sundays as mandated by law).

Stranded motorists would be so desperate for fuel that many of them offered to give me extra money just to provide them any amount of gasoline. The highest I was ever offered was $50. I would never take the money, of course, because I didn't deserve it. I would never have exploited anyone in an emergency situation like that. It also wouldn't have been fair to the rest of my customers who depended on us to sell them the fuel that they needed during our already reduced hours. There was never a shortage of stranded motorists on the Grapevine during this time. It was sad that I could not help them all. I made very few exceptions and helped only the neediest cases - pregnant women, the elderly and those with very young children.

There was a positive spin to all of this, however. We had many opportunities to take our employees on company outings during the gas shortage, since our hours were greatly reduced. I was a member of a sailing club since I was 18 years old, and so I had a great excuse to go sailing with all of the staff to build up employee morale and to aid in stress relief; Lord knows we needed it. We continued to go sailing for many years after the fuel shortage because I discovered that it was very beneficial to our working relationships. We had so much fun bonding and getting to know our each other on a deeper level. It was an added fringe benefit to their job that many of them would never have experienced otherwise.

We would frequently run out of gas during the fuel shortage. When things finally returned to normal, we would still occasionally run out of fuel unintentionally. This time, however, it was because of the new automated tank monitoring system that the oil companies installed. When we did run out, it was usually the oil company's fault because the computer program that runs the system may have misjudged our inventory and/or sales, or there could have been problems at the terminal or with the delivery trucks. It seemed like it only happened on holidays when our fuel sales dramatically increased. The automated system would often fail to realize when (and by how much) our sales would rise because of a holiday or special event. Most gas station volumes slowed down on holiday weekends because everyone would leave town on that Friday. However, because our station was on the same highway that everyone would leave town on, we would always be busy during their holiday weekend pilgrimages.

It was amusing the way our customers would react when we had to tell them that we ran out of gas. They didn't believe it and they thought that we were kidding. They just couldn't imagine that a gas station would ever run out of gas. It was always embarrassing for us when it happened, but more than that, it would cost us a lot of money in lost sales. Some customers would still purchase items in the store, but it was never enough to make up for the lost gasoline sales to our competitor across the street. Fortunately, our rival would inevitably run out of fuel on a holiday also, and then we would get back all of that lost business that we gave them when we ran dry.

Odd-Even Plans Returning As Iran Gas Crunch Mounts

By PETER J. BERNSTEIN

WASHINGTON — Odd-even gasoline rationing may be just around the corner in many states because of the increased likelihood of new oil shortages resulting from turmoil in Iran.

Tomorrow, California will become the first state to resume the odd-even system statewide.

In the East, at least four states — New York, New Jersey, Connecticut and Maryland — have contingency plans ready if officials detect new shortages of gasoline.

In New York, energy officials say Gov. Hugh Carey could reimpose odd-even rationing as a conservation measure even before long gas lines or other signs of shortages appear.

And in New Jersey, state officials say Gov. Brendan Byrne may reinstitute some form of rationing in response to President Carter's recent appeal to gov-

As long as production remains at current levels, Lichtblau says, there's a "tenuous supply-demand balance" in the world. But a cut in Iranian output could trigger a worldwide scramble for oil similar to the one that preceded last spring's gas lines.

So far, there isn't any hard evidence that Iran is planning to cut production, U.S. energy officials say.

But the Carter administration, emphasizing the uncertainty of the situation, is taking advantage of the crisis abroad to gain support at home for its conservation goals.

One U.S. official said the United States will have an oil reduction in 45 to 50 days — after the last tankers arrive from Iran — of 700,000 barrels a day of crude oil.

He said there must be "an early and permanent" effort to reduce energy consumption and eliminate waste.

percent alcohol — to equal 10 percent of the nation's total unleaded gasoline consumption. Currently, it equals less than 1 percent.

However, the view is growing both in and out of government that far sterner measures may be needed to cope with the oil crisis.

Many experts maintain there will be further disruptions of the world's oil supply.

The ferment in Iran, which could degenerate into anarchy or civil war, might impair that nation's ability to produce any oil.

Turmoil in Iran also could spread to other oil-producing states in the Middle East. Although production has been running at high rates, a number of these Middle Eastern countries — including Saudi Arabia — have suggested they might cut down.

Meanwhile, the chaos in Iran is

CHAPTER 4

Things Return to Normal

After gasoline supplies returned to normal, we were able to acquire additional stations. We had one memorable station near Hollywood that was owned by the garage mechanic who wasn't interested in utilizing the gas pumps there, so he subleased them to me. Because of its proximity to the studios, we would frequently meet famous people there. One such person that stands out in my mind was Jack Klugman, from the hit television series, "The Odd Couple" and "Qunicy." He had left his credit card at the station and the cashier didn't notice it quickly enough to return it to him. To my amazement, Jack was listed in the phone book, so I called him. The conversation went something like this:

JACK : Hello?

ME   : Jack!

JACK : Who's this?

ME   : It's Dave.

JACK : Dave who?

ME   : Dave Nassaney, I own the gas station that
           you left your credit card at last night.

JACK : Oh, really? Wow!

ME   : Yea, when can you come by and get it?

JACK : I'll come tomorrow.

ME   : OK, Thanks Jack, we'll see you then.

JACK : OK, bye.

ME   : Bye.

I was so excited that I actually got with speak to the great Jack Klugman (like I've known him for years). I used to tell that story to whoever would listen to me until everyone was sick of hearing it.

More recently in Castaic, I met Jack Palance from the hit movie, "City Slickers". He was pretty old and not in great health at the time but he still had great stature and presence. I asked him if he was really Jack Palance. He said in a very stern voice with piercing eyes, "NO!", and he was pretty grouchy and ornery about it too. His daughter, whom he was traveling with, then whispered to me that it was in fact him and that he was very cantankerous in his old age. He was still very big, and pretty intimidating to look at. I could imagine how Billy Crystal felt in "City Slickers" when Jack told him, "I crap bigger than you!"

In 1983, at my Hollywood station, I had a very memorable employee working for me, his name was Thad Swift. He was in his 70's and drove a 1927 Track-T Classic Roadster built from a kit. He had written a movie script and became obsessed about his science fiction story of an army of alien forces coming to earth to take all of the world's children away from us. The aliens felt we didn't deserve the right to raise our own children because we were always starting wars and killing each other; we would just teach our children to do the same. The extra-terrestrials said that they would only return our children to us if we all reconciled with each other and agreed to sign peace treaties with all of the countries of the world. Emotional and teary-eyed Soviet leaders were actually speaking kindly to their heart-broken American counterparts in order to negotiate a peace on the earth so that they could get all of their beloved children back.

My employee had spent tens of thousands of dollars writing this screen play along with professional renderings designed on a story board. He then spent the last of his monies trying to pitch his movie idea to any producer in Hollywood who would listen to him. Finally running out of cash, he had to work for me just to pay for his living expenses. Even though he was flat broke, he still loved to drive his very expensive Classic Roadster (his only prized possession). He said he would go hungry before he would ever sell that car. Over the years I've always wondered if he was still alive or if he died along with his dreams. Unfortunately, Hollywood is full of stories such as these.

After the gas shortage ended, we all thought that there would be another energy crisis soon because the Middle East was so volatile and the U.S. was so dependent on imported oil. As a result, gas station business goodwill values had soared. I was constantly getting calls from Middle Easterners and brokers who wanted to buy my gas station (any station) and they had suitcases full of cash to pay for them. It was not unusual for these foreigners to pay as much as $500,000 for a gas station lease (which did not include the land or the improvements). Before the fuel shortage, these leases were not worth much, if anything. In a gas shortage, however, profits usually doubled or tripled because of increased margins and reduced expenses from shortened operating hours; thus, the perceived value of station goodwill went through the roof.

Yet, to everyone's surprise, the long- awaited gasoline shortage never really materialized, except for isolated geographic areas due to hurricanes or other natural disasters. However, as of the date of this writing, some are still expecting a true energy crisis that would include a full world-wide fuel shortage in the years to come, brought about by war or natural disaster.

This would be a good place for me to answer two of my most frequently asked questions. The first is, "Are all gasoline brands the same, or are some brands better than others?" The answer is, "That depends." When gas station real estate is owned by an oil company, the chances of a motorist receiving inferior fuel are greatly reduced. The oil companies are very serious about product quality, and it is very difficult for a dealer at these company-owned locations to buy any inferior, non-branded gasoline to add to their inventory. The oil company monitors the dealer's sales and purchases and will terminate their franchise agreement if they are ever caught co-mingling their gasoline with cheaper non-branded fuel.

That being said, you can usually tell which gas stations are independently owned versus which ones are owned by the oil companies. Each company's gas station looks alike and has its own design characteristics. For example, Shell's architecture looks very different from Mobil's; Union 76 looks different from Arco, and so on. The Shell's, Mobil's and Unocal's that look like they all have a similar building design, (and can all be interchanged with one another by just changing the I.D. sign panel) are typically independently owned. Those operators can more easily co-mingle non- branded gas, and may occasionally acquire some bad fuel with water or other contaminates in it. Whenever a dealer buys cheaper gas from an unknown outside source, they will always run the risk of obtaining tainted fuel.

When an oil company has refinery problems, they will often fill up their trucks with one another's fuel; in essence, they co- mingling their gas. However, when they do it, it is not co-mingling because they add their top-secret ingredients to it which magically makes it their very unique brand. So, the short answer to the question is no, gas is gas. Some people will argue with me on this point, however, insisting that their car will only operate on Chevron or Mobil gas without pinging or knocking. I don't have an answer for them. These same people probably claim that they can tell the difference blindfolded between Dasani and Aquafina water. Maybe they need to blindfold their car's headlights the next time they fill it up at a different gas station. □

As far as the question of whether premium gasoline is really better for your car and worth the extra cost, well that depends on your car's personality. Some cars want the extra octane, and will ping and knock if they don't get it. Some drivers believe that an engine will last longer if they use premium gasoline. Look at your owner's manual, it may recommend premium, but not require it. Some think that it will give them better gas mileage. It might, but will that additional savings be worth the extra 20 cents per gallon? Maybe; I never used premium, even when I owned a Lexus, and it would run just fine.

CHAPTER 5

Runaway Big Rigs

There have been a lot of runaway tractor- trailer trucks (otherwise known as big rigs) that have lost their brakes and plowed right into our building as they reached the bottom of the hill. As I mentioned in the previous chapter, there are runaway escape ramps only on the northbound side of Interstate 5 for big rigs whose brakes fail on this very long steep grade. However, Caltrans (they maintain the state's highways) has never built any escape ramps on the southbound side where my gas station sits. In 2001, I wrote them a letter complaining about all of the trucks that have lost their brakes at my off-ramp. The runaway trucks would then continue right into my gas station. I suggested that they install a runaway truck ramp, or a sign saying, "Runaway Trucks – Do Not Exit," since the freeway levels off just after my off-ramp. It was illogical for me to imagine how any driver of a runaway big rig with burning brakes would actually think that it was safe to exit an off-ramp with such a tight turn, and then try to pull into a gas station (of all places). The safest thing for them to have done was to simply continue on the freeway without exiting.

Caltrans did a study as a result of my letter and found that there were not enough accidents at my off-ramp to warrant a runaway truck ramp being built. However, they did remove the guardrails along the off- ramp as a "token of cooperation." That allowed runaway trucks to cross the dividing space of the on/off-ramps to re-enter the freeway. However, the trucks still continued to lose their brakes which made my gas station a potential target for serious accidents. I can remember at least twelve brake related accidents at my location within the last thirty years, a little less than one every two years. I guess that's not enough accidents to install a runaway truck ramp, since nobody has been killed yet.

The worst truck accident at my location took place in the early 1980s. A young truck driver (who didn't speak much English) was riding his brakes down the hill. This made them very hot when he didn't release the brake pedal every now and then to allow them to cool off. After a truck gets past a certain speed, it is impossible to down-shift the gears to aid it in slowing down. By the time the truck arrived at my off-ramp, both rear wheels were smoking and in flames. So, I'm sure this kid thinks to himself, "Where can I steer this flaming runaway tractor-trailer? I know...that gas station over there looks safe." Wow! What an idiot!

In those days, my station consisted of a customer waiting room and two garage bays. I had about ten vending machines in the waiting room and my manager's girlfriend's ten-year- old son happened to be in that room. The truck approached the building doing about 35MPH. The boy saw him coming and freaked. The driver also saw him and turned the cab so sharply to avoid hitting the building that it caused his trailer to tip over from the inertia of the sharp turn.

The trailer then fell onto our glass storefront and brick wall, encroaching three feet into the waiting room causing all the vending machines on that part of the wall to be knocked about like a ball in a pinball machine. The cab continued down its path heading right towards my 500-gallon (above- ground) propane tank. I'm not sure what would happen to a propane tank that was hit by a truck whose brakes were on fire, but I suspect it would not be good.

By the time my manager climbed over the trailer to get into the room to see if the boy was injured, he saw see all the vending machines pushed over to one corner of the room. He called out to the boy, and heard him crying. He climbed over several vending machines to reach the cry and found him in the corner. Three machines had jammed together in such a way as to make a pocket of space without him getting crushed. He was crouched over in the fetal position, badly shaken, but not injured. For many weeks to come he enjoyed telling his story to everyone who came into the station, and anyone else who would listen to him at home.

The funny part about this tragic story was what the driver was hauling. It was a Foster Farms chicken truck with hundreds of live chickens on their way to the slaughter house. As you can imagine, all of the chicken cages that hit the building got smashed and were thrown onto their sides. Some chickens didn't make it, some escaped when their cages came open, and others just laid an egg or two. There were live chickens everywhere running in circles (and a few dead ones).

We helped round up the live ones and decided to put them in the ladies' restroom for safe keeping because it was slightly larger than the men's restroom. After a few minutes we started smelling a familiar aroma like breakfast. It was over 100 degrees that summer day and if you ever wondered if it was possible to fry an egg on the asphalt on a sunny day, the answer is definitely yes. There was breakfast being served everywhere.

As I mentioned earlier, our gas station happened to be a very busy restroom stop because the 27-mile grade above us has no rest areas or populated exits, so it was only a matter of time before a lady would need to use the restroom. Sure enough, a few minutes later I was approached by an elderly lady who asked me if she could please use the restroom. So naturally I told her that it was out of order. She suddenly became irate and started yelling at me, "You gas station owners are all alike! I can never find a restroom on the highway that is not out of order. I don't believe that it's out of order!"

This is actually a pretty typical reaction whenever our restrooms have to be put out of order to service or repair them. It is pretty rare that they are closed for longer than a few minutes. We make sure that they are always clean, well-stocked and in good working condition. We wouldn't have been able to handle the abuse by the customers if they weren't in good working order. They demanded a clean restroom and were pretty upset if they didn't get one.

However, this particular time I calmly looked at her and said, "Madam, please follow me, I will take you to our restroom." So, I took her to the door and invited her to go in. She opened the door and saw about one-hundred chickens on the toilet, the sink, the floor and the counter; they were everywhere. She then looked at me and said, "Oh, I'm very sorry that I doubted you, young man. Please forgive me."

The local newspaper even came by to take some photos of the truck accident and noticed the chickens in the ladies' restroom. We were on the front page of the Newhall Signal the next day. There was a picture looking inside the door of our ladies' restroom with chickens standing everywhere. Underneath the picture was the caption, "Coo Clucks Can."

The other memorable runaway truck accident that stuck in my mind was when a tractor trailer smashed into the wall of our building that borders   my office. It totally demolished my desk and there was rubble everywhere. Thank God that I was not sitting at my desk or I might not have been around to write this book. That accident actually was a blessing in disguise because my cousin, who is a contractor, totally remodeled my office with the insurance money using very attractive paneling, decorative mirrors and a beautiful office desk combination set. We also had the extra room to make it a little larger than it was.

Other dealers were jealous of the size of my beautifully decorated office when they would visit me. Most gas station offices are pretty tiny and ugly, usually having to share the space with cases of oil, soda and potato chips. Our new office was paid for by the driver's insurance company. They didn't blink an eye when they wrote the check because they were so grateful that no one was killed or seriously injured.

On other occasions, the runaway trucks would often overturn while trying to negotiate the tight turn at the off-ramp. The good news was that they never made it into our gas station. The bad news was that it shut down the south-bound off-ramp for most of the day (which just happens to supply 95% of our gas customers). We would lose a lot of money whenever that off-ramp was shut down.

Trucks aren't the only ones smashing into our gas station. One time a lady who thought she was stepping on the brake pedal instead stepped on the accelerator and destroyed a wall just north of our building, taking out our pay phones and two Cal Tran signs. According to my security video, an entire family was in that very spot just seconds before the accident.

CHAPTER 6

Abandoned Vehicles

You can't even imagine all of the aging vehicles that have overheated while attempting to climb the steep grade on the Grapevine, (also known as the Ridge Route) especially in the summer time when temperatures can exceed well over 100 degrees. Most of the cars that just happened to expire at the top of that mountain would inevitably have to coast down the hill under that powerful force called gravity right into my gas station.

They would usually need a little extra push that last few feet across the street onto our property. If I was fortunate enough to see them pushing it before they made it into my driveway, I would strongly encourage them to push their lifeless car across the street to my competitor's gas station instead. I recognized the familiar smell of a fried engine that was deprived of precious oil or water that it so desperately needed for that vehicle to live another day.

It was funny (but also very sad) as the owners of these departed vehicles would usually be in denial about their auto's untimely demise. They just couldn't accept that their car had left them stranded in the middle of nowhere. They were usually going through very difficult circumstances and often broke down and cried. Some were women with small children, some were elderly couples, and some were disabled. They all had one thing in common though. They were all down on their luck, had no money, and now they had no car; it was heartbreaking. We would help some of them by calling a family member to rescue them. Some others we gave a ride to the bus depot. Still others by calling them a cab or helping them call Western Union to have money wired. Sadly, several of them (the unlucky ones) didn't have any friends or family to call.

At that time, the bad news for us was that once their dead car entered onto our property, it was now our responsibility to have it removed. If, however, it was abandoned on the street, then it was the county's responsibility to tow and store it.

If we didn't notice the slow accumulation of these abandoned vehicles, the station would eventually begin to look like a junk yard. Many of those Junkers seemed like they just magically appeared the next morning when the graveyard shift wasn't paying close attention, or when we happened to close down for the night. I would ask my manager that all too familiar question, "Weren't there only two abandoned vehicles on our lot last night? Where did this third one come from?"

The abandoned vehicle problem is actually much better today because the California Highway Patrol (CHP) changed the rules for abandoned vehicles. All a property owner has to do now is to post a sign on their lot that says, "Tow Away, No Parking," that would also include the phone number of who towed it. Towing companies are now able to salvage the abandoned vehicles to a junkyard for scrap metal allowing them to make a profit over and above the towing and storage charges that they incur.

On another day, I came to work after closing the night before and found a very different kind of abandoned vehicle on my property. It was a Cessna light twin-engine personal transport aircraft. I was so excited. I said to myself, "Finally someone abandoned something that I actually want and isn't a piece of junk!" We pushed the aircraft into one of our parking spots and then we went about our daily duties (later forgetting that it was even there). That afternoon I received a call from someone asking if an airplane had been left on our property last night. I told the caller to hold on while I checked. I waited a few minutes and then picked up the phone again to ask him, "What color?"

It turned out that he was flying over our gas station the night before when he discovered that it was losing oil pressure. He looked down to see where he could land and decided to land on The Old Road (which is actually the name of the road in front of our gas station). He made a successful landing and pulled it onto our property. For some reason he did not even bother to leave a note.

I was so disappointed that someone had claimed the aircraft. I was secretly hoping that no one would ever call so that I could take possession of it. After all, they say that possession is nine tenths of the law...don't they? I know...I was just dreaming, and that it wasn't ever likely to happen. I realized that I had to give the plane back and I was very sad about it.

The owner came back to fix the leaky oil hose that day and filled up the crankcase with some fresh oil. He then fired up the engine and it purred like a kitten. He called the Federal Aviation Administration (FAA) to get flight permission to take off from The Old Road. He was on the phone with them for about an hour. They were arguing back and forth; they wanted him to take the wings off and trailer it. He said that he was not going to spend a fortune to do that when he could just take off so easily on this deserted road right in front of my gas station. He finally hung up the phone in frustration and told me that he had to leave immediately.

He fired it up again and started taxiing down The Old Road. He taxied about one-hundred yards when all of a sudden, a CHP vehicle came out of nowhere with lights and sirens blazing as he chased this plane doing about 60 MPH. He finally pulled him over before the plane could take off. He escorted it back to the gas station and explained that the FAA called the CHP because they assumed the pilot might try to take off without FAA permission and wanted him stopped. The owner of the plane then got back on the phone with the FAA for another fifteen minutes.

They finally agreed that if the CHP would escort the plane and stop all traffic on The Old Road, then the FAA would let him legally take off. And that is exactly what happened. Everything was quiet and peaceful once again. I really missed that plane after it was gone, but the owner gave me a coupon for a free flying lesson in appreciation of all the trouble that he caused us (as well as our cooperation in giving him back his plane). I kept that coupon for a very long time, hoping to find the right time to redeem it. Unfortunately, I somehow lost it which made me very sad. I only took one flying lesson in my life when I was 18. It would have been a lot of fun to fly a plane again after so many years.

Besides Junkers, there were also some very expensive vehicles that were abandoned on our property. Those owners fully intended to return to their cars and fix them or tow them away. To my amazement, however, many of them thought that they could just leave their broken vehicle on my property without asking or telling anyone that they left it there. These same people would then come back in one or two weeks and fully expect their vehicle to still be right where they left it. They were then shocked when we told them that their vehicle was towed away, just like the sign on the property said it would be. Most of these cars were abandoned right on top of my underground gasoline storage tanks, which made it impossible for the gasoline tanker driver to drop their fuel into our tanks.

Those tanker drivers tended to be very impatient people. They were on a schedule and had many gas loads to deliver in a short amount of time. The oil companies equipped their tankers with electronic monitoring devices that told their bosses where the drivers were and how long they stopped for. This discouraged dishonest drivers from being lazy and inefficient. If the tanks were blocked by vehicles, they would usually honk their very loud horns while double parked in the center divider of the street. I have actually had a driver leave our location because of this, and as a result, we ran out of gas. It was very important that we kept this area clear of abandoned vehicles, especially when we closed at night. When the vehicles owner finally showed up, I would just give them the name of the towing company so that they could redeem their car in exchange for the towing and daily storage charges.

While we are on the topic of underground storage tanks, I am frequently asked how many gas tanks did I have and how many gallons did they hold? The station has three fiberglass double-walled underground storage tanks. One holds 12,000 gallons and the other two hold 10,000 gallons each for a total of 32,000 gallons. We used to have three products of gasoline delivered to us, but then they devised a way to mix (or blend) the Super (91 octane) and the Regular (87 octane) gas together to produce the Special (mid-grade 89 octane) gasoline. It was a more efficient use of the storage tanks and delivery tankers.

The tanks were rarely filled to capacity because it would have cost over $128,000 to fill them at today's prices. Only 25% of the sales were Super and Special gasoline combined. We usually kept anywhere between 5,000 to 11,000 gallons of Regular and 1,000 to 3,000 gallons of Super in the ground. Each delivery of gasoline came in a 9,000-gallon tanker and cost about $50,000 at today's prices in 2020.

CHAPTER 7

Pricing

I will discuss in this chapter the popular topic of pricing and the role that the oil companies play in that complicated process. If this is a subject that is not of interest to you, or if I lose you half way through this chapter, please feel free to fast-forward a paragraph or two, or just skip this chapter altogether if it is more information than you wanted to hear.

The gas station dealer is an independent businessman who signed a lease and a supply contract with the oil company to sell their gas. The rents that they charge the dealer are excessive by any standard. The oil company's conflict of interest of being both the dealer's landlord and his fuel supplier puts the dealer at a great disadvantage.

Many times, the oil companies would use their power and influence as our landlord to affect our purchasing decisions as our supplier. They do this by implying us how much money we can make on our gas, even though they cannot legally do so. Whenever we would attempt to discuss the topic of unfair pricing with them, they would always say, "I'm sorry, we are prohibited by Federal law from discussing prices with you." They would often get around the legalities by making sure that their illegal threats were always spoken, and never written.

When the oil company used to sell us our motor oil, they would pressure dealers into buying truckloads of it as a personal favor to them. They would imply that if we did them this favor, they would somehow make it up to us. They usually implied that they would lower our rents the next time our lease came up for renewal, or they would put our station at the top of the remodeling list for station upgrades. Dealers who did not buy their truckloads of oil coincidentally found their rents rising and their stations falling into disrepair. Those dealers who bought the truckload deal had to rent a huge cargo container just to store a year's worth of oil on their property. Those same dealers would end up being forced to have a big clearance sale (usually selling it at or below cost) just to get rid of it.

Fortunately, the oil company no longer sells oil directly to the dealer, but instead they exclusively market oil through wholesalers, (often selling it much cheaper than they used to sell it to their own dealers). They would also use similar tactics with our gas purchases. For example, they would say, "You know, we think that you can sell a lot more gas if you would just lower your prices. Don't worry about losing profit margin because you will make up that lost profit in volume." This was an argument that sounded logical on the surface but was not applicable to many locations, including mine.

Our gas station was on a lake resort exit and did not have much of a local trade. Lowering our prices might work in a more competitive location, but not in ours. We tried it many times but ended up pumping the same number of gallons regardless of the price we charged. People came to us because they needed gas and there was nowhere else to go with an easy on and off-ramp. The oil company representatives would make subtle oral threats that if we didn't lower our prices, they would have to get their extra income from our location by raising our rent. I actually heard one oil company executive say that they would get their money from us one way or another. He meant that if he didn't get it from the increased sales of our gas, he would get it from the increased rents they would charge us, or from the savings to them in deferred maintenance that never seemed to get performed at our location. In other words, they would punish us. These kinds of threats were very common and also very illegal because they are a form of price controls by a wholesaler on an independent retailer.

In fact, we saw our rents go up from $2,500 to $3,500 to $6,250 and then 10% a year from that point on with a $12,000 cap (which we quickly reached). These increases had nothing to do with our profitability, lack of profitability, the economy or even inflation. The rent increases were just mandated into our new leases that we would sign every three years. Our oil company supplier insisted on making a 10% (later raised to 12%) rate of return on their gas station assets for their stockholders in rents no matter what. The fact that they did this not only to me, but to all dealers made it legal (treating everyone the same and not discriminating).

No other industry saw this type of rent increases. The dealer has always struggled to survive in a climate of razor-thin shrinking profit margins. Many dealers today are forced to make the same profit per gallon (between six to twelve cents) that they were making forty years ago, yet every expense has doubled, tripled or even quadrupled. Expenses like insurance, wages, rents, credit card fees, maintenance, supplies,workers compensation, taxes, environmental fees, etc.

To ensure that the dealers make only what the oil companies want them to make, the oil companies devised something called zone pricing. This means that the oil company can arbitrarily determine price zones and set a different wholesale price for different dealers based on their zone. The boundaries of these price zones or the stations they are comparing us to are not known to us because they keep their identity a secret from the dealers. Their company-run stations (often just down the block from our stations) would regularly post retail prices below our cost, pressuring us further to lower our prices to compete with them and lose profit margin.

This was just another way that the oil company could punish the dealer by controlling his profit margin and raising the dealer's wholesale price independent of any other dealer's price. They could even put a station in its very own price zone. That means that even though my competitor (just three miles down the road from me) happened to have a lower retail and wholesale price than mine, the oil company could keep my prices higher because they would not take into account those stations that they made sure were not in my price zone.

All of this is a very complicated computer model and perfectly legal for the oil companies to do, because the courts have determined that they cannot single out and screw one particular dealer. So instead, they have decided to screw all of us dealers equally. As long as they treated us all the same, then they were not breaking the law. The oil companies have their own paid political lobbyists to ensure that the laws were written in their favor (after heavily contributing to their political campaigns, of course).

That is why one gas station can charge one price and the same brand of gas down the block can charge ten cents higher or lower, yet they would both be making the same profit margin because one is being charged a higher or lower wholesale price for the same gas. Can you imagine if McDonalds were charging its Beverly Hills restaurant franchises more for their beef than their stores in Pacoima (or even the one down the block) just because they could? This is what is happening to the gas station dealers. It just so happens that our brand of gas has historically had the highest price over its competition since they merged with another oil giant over a decade ago, further reducing competition. It was very common afterwards for my station's wholesale cost of gas to be at least ten cents higher than my competitor right across the street, putting me at a great competitive disadvantage.

Many people ask me why the retail price of gas seems like it goes up on the very same day that a news event would suggest that a price increase is coming. For example, if Israel is threatening war with Iran over its nuclear aspirations. This would make the uninterrupted supply of oil more uncertain. So, you might ask, "Why would the gas stations immediately respond to such a news event since the fuel in their underground storage tanks is not subject to the news event that would cause that price to immediately increase?" The same question would also apply to the refinery's gas in its storage tanks, and the oil tankers anchored off shore with the cheaper fuel still in its hulls.

The simple answer is because they can, and so they do. When prices were rising, I would raise my prices immediately upon getting the increase from our supplier, even though the cheaper gas was still in my underground tanks. That improved our profit margin (which always needed improvement). I suspect the oil companies and refineries are the same way. It was an opportunity for them to improve their profits (not that their profits needed any improving like ours did). They raised our price even though the gas in their storage tanks was still at the cheaper price. We were simply passing the cost on to the consumer sooner rather than later.

Now when the gas prices were going down, no one was in a hurry to lower their prices, not the oil companies and not the dealers. I'm just being truthful and honest here. I know you probably think this is very unfair, but just consider that most gas stations are making the same twelve cent per gallon profit margin on their gas that they were making forty years ago, yet every one of their expenses has increased many times over.

I was very blessed to have had a gas station in what is called an inelastic demand location (along a busy freeway interstate in a lake resort area with little or no competition). What that means is that the higher the price that I charge (or anyone charges) for an item (like gasoline), the less likely that the demand for that product will decrease. In its simplest definition, inelastic demand means that it takes more of a price movement to effect a change in demand. Elastic demand means that it takes less of a price movement to effect that same change in demand.

It is interesting to note that even in the wake of higher gasoline prices, Americans have not embraced carpooling or public transportation yet (at least not in the short run). Although a study found that 28% of consumers did buy less gasoline than usual since the rise in gas prices. By implication, 72% of consumers have not reduced their gasoline purchases.

If a gas station in a downtown area has twenty gas stations in a one-mile radius of it and raises their price ten cents per gallon, it would be very easy for a consumer to simply get their gas from a nearby competitor who has not yet raised their price. That area has a very elastic demand for gas. In other words, the more you raise or lower the price of gas there, the more sensitive the consumer is to react quickly and equally to that change.

Ninety percent of gas stations find themselves in this type of marketplace, and tend to be not as profitable as the other ten percent who are in inelastic demand locations (that are on lonely stretches of highway with little or no competition) where there are fewer opportunities to purchase a competitor's gas. These gas stations are doing much better financially than the majority of stations.

I am always asked if anyone really makes any money selling gasoline any more. The answer is that it depends on your location, location, location. It is not that the ten percent of gas stations that are in great locations, (and can charge what they need to survive) are charging too much for their gas. It's that the ninety percent of the rest of the gas stations in very competitive locations cannot charge what they need to in order to continue in business. They are in fact charging too little for their gas, and are in poor financial health as a result. That is why thousands of gas stations have just disappeared over the last forty years in this country. They couldn't charge the price that they needed to because of too much competition.

Only the strong locations have survived, and the weak ones continue to vanish. But fewer gas stations are bad for competition. About fifteen years ago when the oil companies started merging with each other, instead of the twelve oil companies (and as many refineries) supplying Los Angeles, only 5 are now left. With so few refineries still around, it only takes one refinery shutting down for maintenance or responding to an accident to cause prices to skyrocket in that isolated area.

At the time of this writing, the price of gas went up fifty cents per gallon due to a fire at a Chevron Refinery in San Francisco and an electrical outage at the ExxonMobil refinery in Torrance. We are in a very vulnerable position as a result of fewer gas stations, fewer refineries and fewer oil companies in the marketplace. Look for these price hikes to replicate again and again as a result.

There is an intersection in Santa Clarita on Interstate 5 affectionately called "Hamburger Hill." It is a one-mile radius with about fifty places to get fast food. They just keep crowding into this area thinking it is a great place to put another fast-food restaurant. But for some reason they don't realize that the food wars that are a result of this over-saturation in such a small area have made the hamburger business less profitable for everyone there.

We have all become accustomed to the fast-food dollar menus that command little if any profit for the retailer. The profit pie just keeps getting smaller and smaller, which doesn't leave much profit for many retailers to survive on. That is great for the consumer in the short run, but bad for them in the long run when many restaurants and gas stations start to go out of business during a prolonged recession (which in turn means less competition and higher prices).

The Government used to protect the small independent entrepreneur from unfair anti-trust policies by giant multinational corporations, but with the implementation of the North Atlantic Free Trade Association (NAFTA), our politicians have left the small businessperson to fend for themself.

One popular and creative way that gas stations are becoming more profitable is for them to implement cash/credit pricing (charging more for credit and debit cards and less for cash). This adds the much-needed profit to help dealers pay for those ever-increasing credit card processing fees. These cards are becoming more and more expensive for dealers to accept as the price of gas continues to rise. On average, we paid a 2% fee to the card processor which increased as the price of gas rose. We used to pay about $2500 a month in the 1970's when gasoline was much cheaper. We then paid upwards of

$8000 to $9000 a month for the same processing services when gas prices reached their height. The only reason for that higher fee was that the same 2% processing fee was later calculated on the higher gas price. It seemed only fair that credit and debit card holders should help pay that extra cost so that we could continue to stay in business while providing them with a very valuable convenience. This is a problem peculiar only to gas stations because they sell a commodity that has very extensive price fluctuations.

However, after hearing many complaints from our customers about being charged the credit price for using their debit (ATM) cards, we considered making ATM usage at our station the same as cash (even though we were charged to process them also). Customers just didn't get it. They believed that ATM was the same as cash (and to them it was). But to us, ATM was the same as credit because it cost us to process them as well. Actually, we were only charged a 1.5% fee on the debit transaction while we were charged a 2.2% fee to process a credit transaction.

My plan was to make ATM the same as cash to the customer, and hope that giving them the choice would increase my ATM usage and decrease my credit card usage. The savings from the lower ATM fees would hopefully help defer the costs from the higher credit card fees. The result was that our fees went down and the ATM users were happy that they received the cash price. This seemed like a good compromise.

CHAPTER 8

Freeway Closures

We were a twenty-four-hour station, however, in the winter months we would sometimes close at midnight because it was just so slow. It would cost more to pay the employee on duty along with the electric bill than it would to just close down. The profit that we would generate on the gas and snack sales would not even cover those two expenses. Another reason we would shut down during the graveyard shift (10pm to 6am) was due to road closures that would occur on the Grapevine as a result of snow and ice, brush fires, accidents, and road maintenance.

However, the first day or two of the road closures were usually very busy for us. People were ushered off the freeway by the CHP and would start roaming all around the tiny town of Castaic. They would eventually find their way to our gas station to buy some coffee, gas and of course to use the restroom. After news of the road closure would reach their car radios, people would tend to stay away and use alternate routes. Business then became very slow until the roads reopened. If it was a severe storm expected throughout the night and well-advertised on the radio, we would then just shut down for the night.

It was very frustrating when the freeway closed due to snow or brush fires because every thirty seconds someone would ask the same questions over and over again: "Is the freeway closed? What do I do now? How long will it be closed? Are there any alternate routes? Will it be open soon? Should I wait?" All night long we were asked these questions. In order to keep our sanity, I would draw them a map and post it at the cash register and the front door showing the alternate routes going north. Highway 126 will detour along to the coast and Highway 14 will detour up through Palmdale and Lancaster. Then cutting back across to meet Interstate 5 again would put between one to three extra hours onto their detour. The map that I drew, however, didn't really help to diminish the questions. The stranded motorists still asked us those same questions. To again keep our sanity and to stop asking myself why these people can't read the sign (or even see the sign), I would just point to the map I drew without saying a word. "Oh, I see. Thank you very much," they would finally say.

The elevation at the top of the hill in Frasier Park is slightly over 4100 feet and is subject to snow and ice in the winter season. Many motorists from the east coast will joke about how quickly the CHP shuts down the freeway just because of a little ice or a few inches of snow that will fall onto the roadway. They are used to driving in blizzards back east, so they just can't believe how California motorist don't know how to drive in icy and snowy conditions. According to the Highway Patrol, it only takes one big rig to skid out of control and block this major north-south artery. That makes the CHP all too willing to close the freeway for safety's sake.

Sometimes in the winter (during one of those proverbial perfect storms) all of the roadways going north seem to unavoidably be shut down all at the same time. Interstate 5 & Highway 14 would close due to snow. Highway 126 & 101 would close due to mudslides from heavy rains (since it is never cold enough at their lower elevations to snow). The other roads may close due to a multi-car pile-up as a result of heavy fog or a big rig accident. When this would happen, people would tend to camp out at my gas station. After their initial coffee, snack and gas purchase, they would just wait for the freeway to reopen - however long it took. When it finally did reopen, only vehicles with chains were allowed to proceed (and we would sell a lot of tire chains). Sometimes if we were scheduled to close and we had nobody who could babysit all those stranded motorists, we would just lock up the building and the pumps and leave all those people marooned on our property.

When they finally reopened the freeway, it would take about an hour for the southbound traffic to reach us from the other side of the mountain. We would then get slammed with customers all exiting at our off ramp for gas, coffee, and restrooms. The restroom line would be very, very long. Customers would tell us tales of how they were stranded at the top of the mountain for four hours in their car. Their cars couldn't move anywhere in the middle of a blizzard until Caltrans plowed the snow from the freeway and escorted a herd of them to my station. Their cars would be loaded up with snow from the storm. Snowball fights would spontaneously erupt on our lot from the playful motorists who were very happy to be back in civilization again.

Every now and then I would take my wife up north to Visalia or Clovis in Kern and Fresno Counties to visit her family. I will never forget what it was like when I got stuck for the first time as a motorist on the other side of the Grapevine. It was much worse than getting stuck at my off ramp because the southbound traffic was usually heavier than the north bound traffic for some reason. There were easily five- hundred cars in that tiny town called Grapevine with only three gas stations and two restaurants - and not much else.

There were lines for everything, and nobody knew when the freeway would re-open. Frantic motorists had to catch a plane, a wedding, a funeral, a ball game, visit their mother in the hospital; you name it. All were stressed out and were not handling the situation very well. I even overheard someone say that they were going to take some back dirt roads that were normally closed to the general public. He mentioned that he was a firefighter and knew where all the dirt access roads were located. It was quite funny for me to see the employees at these gas stations all stressed out with the crowds of people asking them the same questions over and over again that they would ask us at our gas station. I knew exactly what they all were going through.

I then found myself having to make the same decision that all of those people had to make. "Do I wait here for the road to reopen or do I take a detour?" After much deliberation with myself and others, I decided to wait it out. It just didn't make any sense for me to drive all night long using some detour that keeps me in stressful traffic. Instead, I could just relax, enjoy a nice leisurely dinner and still have some time to take a nap. It turned out that I made the right decision because the road reopened in ninety minutes after Cal Trans plowed the snow and the CHP escorted us over the mountain. I love it when a plan comes together.

CHAPTER 9

Restroom Stories

When I took over the Castaic gas station back in 1979, I was amazed at the sheer number of people who used our restrooms. I was told that the original building plans for this gas station back in 1967 included an official travel center that comprised of multiple toilet stalls, urinals and a large customer lobby. However, because the station was over budget at that time, the engineering department in their infinite wisdom decided that cuts were needed, and that they should come from constructing smaller restrooms. As a result, only a single toilet was installed in each tiny rest room. This meant that our customers would forever be waiting in long lines to visit the toilet at this gas station.

It seemed like there was always a restroom line in our mini-mart. In order for our employees to even use the toilet (or even to clean it) we also had to wait in line, usually with a mop and spray bottle in hand. We would have to cut into the front of the line to expedite us getting in and out quickly. Customers typically reacted by asking us why we had to clean it at the exact moment that they were next in line. We would try to explain how we only had a minute or so away from the cash register, and that we have to take advantage of that minute to clean the rest room, since the next opportunity could be hours away. This explanation did little to ease their discomfort as they did the familiar rest room dance.

There are so many stories that I can tell you about our restrooms (and the people who used them) that I just don't know where to begin. Just when we thought that we had seen it all, we were amazed beyond belief once again. The rest room story that I think tops our list was when someone told us that there was a man who was lying on the floor in the men's room. They thought he was sick or something and that we should check him out. It turned out that the man had actually died in there. If that wasn't bad enough, the fact that it took the third customer walking around his body before we were finally notified by somebody that he was in there, was just incredibly unbelievable! I guess the other two people who walked around his body to use the toilet were just too focused on relieving themselves to be aware or concerned. After the ambulance came, we found out that the man had been dying of AIDS. He just happened to be in our restroom when he took his last breath and expired.

On another occasion, a lady complained that the rest room door had been locked for a long period of time. When the cashier opened the door with a key, she found a naked man asleep on the floor with his clothes all bundled up under his head using them as a pillow. She nudged him with her foot and told him to get up. He wouldn't, so she called the sheriff. When they came to investigate, they found that his friends were also asleep in their car and were all under the influence of drugs as well. He took them all to jail and impounded their car, since it was full of illegal drugs.

On a lighter note, many of the people who used our restrooms were very messy. Sometimes the women were worse than the men, but usually the men were messier than the women. Our employee's top complaint was that the men don't flush the toilet, and that they pee all over the floor and the toilet seat. I tried to mitigate this by installing signs. One sign read, "WE AIM TO KEEP THIS RESTROOM CLEAN. YOUR AIM WILL HELP." Another   read,   "MEN, LISTEN TO   YOUR MOTHER. FLUSH THE TOILET."

The next most common complaint by our cashiers was that

Hispanics from Mexico who were not familiar with the modern American toilet didn't know that our plumbing could accept toilet paper without backing up (unlike Mexican toilets). As a result, they would deposit their used toilet paper in the trash container, not in the toilet. As you would guess, this did not make for a very pleasant aroma in the rest room. We also had signs translated into Spanish, "Please do not put toilet paper in the trash can. Put it in the toilet instead." In fact, we had notes all over the restroom (maybe a little too many), but every note addressed an important issue. The problem became a little better, but not much. Maybe the real problem was that some people just couldn't read. Then we took a picture of our rest room when it was trashed, and another picture of it cleaned up, and posted right above the toilet (where we had their undivided attention and they couldn't miss it) for a more visual message.

Finally, we had to do something drastic. We found a company called Nic-O-Lok who makes a lock that requires a quarter to be deposited into a coin box attached to the door knob to open the rest room door. They claimed that it not only would keep our restroom cleaner, but that we would also make the money needed to help pay for vandalism and the necessary paper products. Since we used almost $1,000 worth of toilet paper and seat covers during our busiest months, we tried it.

The first month we took in $2,000 in quarters, but half of the people were really upset with us. They didn't think that we should charge them to use the restroom if they were buying gas. The state legislature even passed a law saying that gas stations on the highway had to provide a public restroom to its customers. It was confusing the way they worded the law, however. How can it be a public restroom if it was only for your customers? Thankfully, Nic-O-Lok had a solution. They provided us with tokens that we gave to customers who thought that they shouldn't have to pay (about half of them). The other half using the restrooms were actually very thankful for our conveniently located facilities, and realized how hard it was to maintain them on the highway (especially when there were no other facilities for twenty- seven miles). They gladly paid twenty-five cents to use them. Some even paid us more because they said they had a lot of family members using it.

Those other customers that we gave the tokens to were clueless as to what it actually took for us to provide them with a clean, law saying that gas stations on the highway had to provide a public restroom to its customers. It was confusing the way they worded the law, however. How can it be a public restroom if it was only for your customers? Thankfully, Nic-O-Lok had a solution. They provided us with tokens that we gave to customers who thought that they shouldn't have to pay (about half of them). The other half using the restrooms were actually very thankful for our conveniently located facilities, and realized how hard it was to maintain them on the highway (especially when there were no other facilities for twenty-seven miles). They gladly paid twenty-five cents to use them. Some even paid us more because they said they had a lot of family members using it.

Those other customers that we gave the tokens to were clueless as to what it actually took for us to provide them with a clean, vandal-free and fully stocked restroom. They felt that if they were putting $50 or $100 worth of gas into their car, then they were entitled to use a free restroom. They were the ones who took one look at the restroom coin device and said (with an attitude in their tone) something like, "I have to pay for the restroom?" or "I'm getting gas, do I still have to pay?" Sometimes they said nothing. They would just get this look on their face, or they would do an about face and storm out of the store muttering to themselves. We would try to tell those people before they reached the front door that we provided free tokens for them. That usually changed their whole demeanor. Their face would light up; they would smile and be happy again. They just wouldn't read the sign on the door, "Customers, request a free token".

After we started giving tokens to those customers who would ask for them, we would still make between $600 to $900 a month from those who didn't mind paying to use the rest room. This just about paid for the toilet paper products used and for the vandalism suffered. These numbers actually would have been two to three times higher if so, many people didn't just catch the door when someone was leaving (usually when there was a long line).

I still thought that it was only fair that everybody should contribute a quarter for a clean, fully stocked, vandalism-free restroom, but apparently only half of the customers seemed to agree with me. After all, "The customer is ALWAYS right!" I was always grateful for some very nice people that would come up to the cashier afterwards and give us a quarter or more, especially upon reading the sign that we strategically placed right in front of the toilet that they couldn't miss as they did their business. It read as follows:

WE APPRECIATE YOUR BUSINESS!!

For those of you who paid twenty- five cents to use this restroom, we sincerely THANK YOU! It is not our intention to upset you in any way by installing coin devices on our restrooms. On the contrary, we sincerely want to be able to supply you with the cleanest, best stocked restroom possible for a gas station.

This gas station restroom is one of the most heavily used on the interstate. We are at the base of a twenty-seven- mile grade that has absolutely NO populated exits or restroom services. As a result, we have as many as 300 to 1000 toilet users in a twenty-four-hour period whose bladders are on "full".

It is a full-time job keeping this restroom clean, well- stocked with paper products, and vandalism free. Installing a coin device simply helps us to afford the very high cost of maintaining it. It easily costs five times as much to maintain it than most other gas stations that are not on a busy highway like Interstate 5, which connects three countries, and three U.S. states on a non-stop divided freeway.

Thank you for understanding our plight, and for not being upset with us. We are doing our best with what we have and can afford. Please let us know if this restroom needs attention in any way. We look forward to seeing you again. Know that your quarter will insure you a clean restroom on your next visit. We have all had the horror of visiting a "restroom from hell", and assure you that will never happen here. If you ever are short of change, we will be happy to supply you with a complimentary token.

The Management.

We found that this note placed right over the toilet (where we had a couple minutes of their undivided attention) made all the difference in the world. They may have been angry going into the restroom, but they would often come out very understanding and empathetic toward our plight. Many would give us an extra dollar or two just because it was so neat and clean; they appreciated that we allowed them to use it.

Some of my employees didn't understand my logic, and wanted to know why we were putting them through the extra burden of having to explain the coin devices to the customers. They asked me why I didn't just raise everything in the store an extra five or ten cents to replace the rest room income. I actually thought about this a lot and I felt that it was important that the customers knew that our restrooms were provided to them at a great sacrifice and cost to us, and that they should be appreciated. We did notice that the restrooms were being kept a lot cleaner by the customers since the coin devices were installed. I think this is because it forced them to think about what it actually took for us to keep them clean, vandal-free and fully stocked. It was an area in the business that I always felt should pull its own weight in contributing to the profit pool.

I know I seemed a little fanatical about the restrooms back then (and even now). Someone even jokingly compared me to the soup Nazi on Seinfeld. They called me the restroom Nazi. I was passionate about keeping our rest rooms clean because I would see on a daily basis people destroying them. We were not their mothers, and we shouldn't have had to clean up after them when they neglected to observe the simplest rules of hygiene.

After all was said and done, I don't think anybody changed their minds on whether they thought that our restrooms should or should not have had coin devices on them. There were already numerous restrooms that have either closed down or were not properly maintained on the highways because business owners just didn't want to put up with the headaches of maintaining them anymore. Even the State of California shut down most of their rest areas on the freeways for the same reason. Just like the demise of full service at the pump, post-pay for gas, free road maps, and free air and water, I believe the free public toilet will be a thing of the past because of the high costs associated with it at freeway rest stop locations. A clean restroom is a very valuable and rare commodity on the highway. "If you clean it, they will pay."

One day, I heard someone banging on the

men's room door. I asked him (speaking through the door) what was wrong. He said he couldn't get out because the lock was jammed. I looked and noticed   that someone had jammed two quarters in the slot and as a result the handle wouldn't turn to open the door. I tried to pry the quarters out of the slot while the man waited patiently in that tiny restroom. I finally got it out and he was able to leave. I apologized to him and told him that it had never happened before. Then five minutes later it happened again, but no quarter was jammed in the slot this time, so I just opened the door for him with my key and let him out. When a third man got trapped in there minutes later, I was curious as to what was causing the trouble, so I went in there with him. A split second before the door slammed shut, I knew I had just made a serious mistake. I was now feeling a bit awkward locked in the restroom with a customer, and we both couldn't get out. I had just come onto my shift and the person I was relieving was about to go home. I was very fortunate that he was still there, however he couldn't hear my banging on the door.

If this had happened when I was alone, I would have been at the mercy of any customer who just happened to walk in to use the men's room. I would have had to explain to him (through the locked door) to put a quarter in the slot to get me out. If the customer happened to be dishonest, he or she could have cleaned out the entire place with no one to stop them.

I had my cell phone with me so I thought I could call the store phone. The only trouble was that my cell phone service did not have reception in my restroom since it was in a metal building. The customer offered me his phone that happened to be with a different provider, and fortunately it worked. I was able to call my co-worker to get us out of there. What a dummy I was getting myself locked in the rest room when I knew that a customer was already trapped in there. Duh!

Sometimes going to the rest room would cause some of our more easily distracted customers to forget that the gas nozzle was still in their gas tanks. For example, they would begin to fill up their car, and then come inside to use the rest room while their nozzle was latched on automatic. After using the rest room, they would then go back to their car and just drive away – causing the nozzle to separate from the hose. The hoses are designed to reconnect. However, the environmental rules say that unless the dealer is certified in vapor recovery nozzle repair (which many are not because it is expensive and time consuming), we were not allowed to reconnect it ourselves. We had to call a service man who charged

$99 to reinstall it and then another $49 to test it for vapor leaks. Sometimes there was nozzle damage when it hit the ground costing another $300. The hose also may have been damaged or stretched costing another $150. In a worst-case scenario, that customer could be looking at a bill of $700 (if everything needed to be replaced including the break-away). However, the average cost to the customer or their auto insurance company was usually about $350.

If we were lucky enough to actually catch the customer before they drove away (or they were actually honest enough to come back in and admit to doing it), then we would charge the customer's credit card or bill their auto insurance company. It seems like it would take an idiot to forget to remove the nozzle from their car, however I have done it twice myself. I did it once at another gas station and once at my own location. There is only one supplier for this equipment which is why it is very expensive. Customers usually get upset when told that they will be charged for the damage. We try to explain to them that it is like any other property damage accident where their automobile hits and damages someone else's property. If they don't pay us, we would have to report their license number to the Sheriff (if we were lucky enough to get that information).

One day, I attended a voice-over workshop just for fun and learned some cool character voices and accents. I produced my own comical commercials to remind customers at the pumps to, "Please remember to replace the nozzle in the hanger BEFORE you drive away!" It plays every 2 minutes, interrupting the music from our iPod. Some of the funny accents I did in the commercials were: Brooklyn, German, Italian, Russian, English, Irish, Jamaican, French, Elvis, Mr. Miyagi (from the Karate Kid), the Godfather, and Danny DiVito. I would I entice our customers to, "Come inside the mini mart and try our triple shot mocha. We even have a drive- thru." It was a lot of fun doing it, and everyone would ask us if it was rough having to listen to those commercials every 2 minutes. After a while, we just tuned it out. Of course, I never got tired of hearing my own voice. LOL

CHAPTER 10

Unforeseen Situations

It didn't take me long to realize that our particular location was in a very unusual spot for people getting stranded without gas, money and even sometimes without a working vehicle. The brutal hills and rugged terrain of the Grapevine/Ridge Route continues to take its toll on cars and drivers alike.

The sudden rise and drop in altitude (1499 feet to 4160 feet above sea level) can cause a car's engine to run very poorly as it is deprived of the oxygen needed for it to run smoothly. The summer heat also causes vehicles to overheat as they climb the steep grade. If the driver doesn't pull over before their car's cooling system starts to overheat, the vehicle can blow a head gasket or crack an engine block; both very expensive repairs. We used to be very busy servicing overheated cars before our garage was converted into a convenience store. The most common cause of overheating was leaky radiator hoses, stuck thermostats, or clogged radiators.

It was easy summer money repairing these cars while the high temperatures persisted, but then as things cooled off, so did the demand for auto repairs. It was difficult providing enough work to keep our mechanic busy. That's when we decided to convert the garage into a convenience store. As a result, our profits increased in the store, and our overhead decreased by closing the garage. People never brought back a Twinkie the way they would bring back a repair job that wasn't right.

The higher elevations were very rough on the drivers also. It would build up a painful pressure in their ears, making it difficult for them to hear well. When they would complain that they couldn't hear us, we would suggest that they squeeze their nose and blow, in order to pop their ears back open. They were so thankful, since many have of them had never heard of that little trick before.

A day never seemed to go by without someone coasting into our gas station that had just run out of gasoline and money. We would often help them out by giving them some gas to get them on their way again. However, we quickly realized that we could not afford to keep doing that every day. Many would promise to pay us back but only about one out of a hundred ever did. Maybe they forgot, maybe they never could afford it, maybe they just couldn't find the gas station, or maybe they lost our address, who knows?

We eventually came up with a bartering system. We would ask the stranded motorists if they had anything to leave as collateral to ensure that they would later come back for it. We would figure what the item was worth new, and then deduct half that value. We would then deduct another half to ensure that we could resell it easily, and not lose any money if they never came back to redeem it. Some items were really cool, and I would often wish that they would never come back for them, like an aircraft, for example, as well as watches, rings, laptops, speakers, skill saws, tools, chain saws, iPods, iPads, etc.

After a while though, our station started looking like a Sanford and Son garage sale (that television show in the 1970's about an amusing junk yard owner and his son). It became obvious to us that we could not continue to allow the station to be cluttered with other people's junk. We simply did not have the room for it, and it also made the store appear cluttered and unprofessional looking. We would still help out stranded motorists as we felt led, we just couldn't help everyone. Fortunately, many were able to call their friends or relatives from our phone, asking to wire them some money via Western Union. People were so appreciative of our kindness that they often sent cards and letters thanking us for our generosity. We posted them all over the wall outside the restroom area where people would enjoy reading them to pass the time while they waited in line. It was a nice feeling to help someone who was stranded. I have been stranded once or twice before, and I know the feeling of helplessness that can often come from being marooned in the middle of nowhere.

People would also lose things at our gas station. They would leave their stuff on the counter, in the restroom, and on top of the gas pumps; things like cell phones, wallets, credit cards, driver's licenses, keys, suitcases, backpacks, gas caps, etc. We always returned the items if we knew where to send them, but many times, there was no address or phone number left with the lost article in order to contact them. Cash was always returned when possible. The individuals that we contacted were usually shocked to get their lost items back, and sometimes they sent us a reward. I have lost my wallet a few times over the years, and it usually gets returned to me. I like to think that it's because I always return lost articles back to their owners. Some call that Karma. I just call it following the Golden Rule; "Do unto others the way you would want others to do unto you."

There were also a few times when I felt that God was leading me to give a certain person some money, or to give another one some gas or some food. They were so appreciative; God was always given the credit for these spiritual encounters. I like to believe that we have drastically changed some people's lives for the better as a result of them wandering into our gas station, and that God was definitely orchestrating it. I believe we were put at the bottom of that hill for a reason, and that reason was to have God bless those individuals that happened to pull into our driveways with a need. I'm just not sure if I was faithful 100% of the time, and that I didn't inadvertently turn away somebody in need that He had sent for me to bless. Sometimes it was tempting for me to miss a golden opportunity to bless someone, especially if I was in a hurry or was too quick to judge that person by the way they looked, smelled or acted.

However, there was another type of visitor that would periodically drop by my gas station. These people were unprincipled and immoral con-artists whose main goal was to rip off unsuspecting cashiers up and down the highway. I am constantly amazed at how these dishonest individuals have no conscience or morals. They can bilk dumb or unsuspecting cashiers (including me---but only once) out of millions of dollars of cash at gas stations, convenience stores and other retailers every single day. Here is how it works.

The scam artist would come in and try to confuse the cashier by doing multiple transactions at once. For example, they may buy a pack of gum for one dollar, and as the cashier would give them their change for a ten- dollar bill, the con would interrupt the cashier in the middle of his or her counting and say something like, "Oh, I'll tell you what, give me back that ten that I just gave you, I don't want all these small bills after all."

If the con can get the cashier to stop counting the change back to them, then the short change artist has just implemented the first step of the con. Once the cashier stops counting, he or she becomes confused. The scam artist is now in control of the transaction, and will then start to tell the cashier what to do. The con would continue to say things like, "Here, let me add these ten ones to my ten- dollar bill that I gave you, and just give me my twenty back. The confused and bewildered cashier usually won't realize that the ten dollars bill the con was talking about was not the scam artist's money, it was the cashiers. A cashier could easily lose fifty or sixty dollars from a good con before they ever knew what hit them.

The con usually waits until the cashier is very busy and the line at the cash register is long enough to improve his chances of confusing and intimidating the clerk. He may also have another person who would cause a distraction that further confuses the cashier. A worker doesn't really learn their lesson until it actually happens to them. Google "short change scam artist" and you will see an amazing video demonstration of how easily it is done.

We would also be approached by vendors selling things out of the back of their trucks. Fruit, perfume, cologne, steaks, lobsters, tools, clothing, you name it. They always have a story of how they were making a delivery and their buyer didn't want it. They would explain how they really couldn't get back to the factory for a few days, so they needed to either sell it to me for half off, or else it would spoil in their truck. The items were usually cheap and not worth what anyone would pay for them.

I made that mistake one time and actually bought several boxes of frozen steaks. They were the toughest steaks that I ever tried to eat in my life. As a general rule, I try not to buy anything that someone would sell out of the back of their car or truck.

On a much sadder note, a very depressing thing happened at our gas station one day. I was working at the cash register and I heard a bunch of sirens pass my station going north, then after about 20 minutes I heard them again going in the opposite direction. About 30 minutes later I heard them coming toward me from the south once more. I looked out the window and saw a pickup truck limping along very slowly on 4 flat tires. He was being followed by about 20 CHP and Sheriff's vehicles. The truck's tires were all coming off of their rims and the driver couldn't go any further. It finally stopped right in front of my station. There had to be at least 20 guns pointed at the driver as they shouted out to him on a megaphone to put his hands on the wheel in plain sight. They next thing I heard was gunfire. I thought that they shot him, but then I noticed that all of the officers had relaxed and put down their guns. It turned out that the driver had shot himself in the head. They pulled him out of his car and laid him on the street with a yellow tarp over his bloody body.

I later found out that he had lived around the corner from the gas station and was probably a customer of ours. He apparently was in rehab for a drug problem and became depressed because he was struggling to stay clean. He told his wife that he was going to commit "suicide by cop" and then he drove off in his truck with his gun. His wife then called the police.

The cops lost no time catching up to him and chased his truck several miles north. They continued to pursue him several more miles south, and then north again to my gas station. Now it just so happened that the bus stop was also at this intersection, so when his son got off the bus from school, he was shocked to discover his dad's truck right there (along with his body next to it) covered with a yellow tarp. It's such a tragedy when someone takes their own life, especially for those that they left to pick up the pieces of their existence, and in many cases, to actually clean up the mess that they left behind.

On another occasion, a very nice gentleman who had been a great customer of ours for over 25 years took his own life because of health issues that he was going through. He told a friend that he didn't want to be a burden to his family any longer, so he decided to put a bullet through his head while he was in his motorhome. You can only imagine the cost and the toll to his family (that he did not want to burden) of cleaning up the mess that he left behind in their motorhome. This behavior simply demonstrates that these people were not thinking clearly when they were in their depressed states of mind. They often ended up causing more pain to those they loved than they ever imagined possible.

We have seen hundreds of people get stopped by the police as they would pull into our gas station (sometimes at gunpoint). We would watch them block our pumps as the police handcuffed them, had their cars searched and impounded, and then hauled them off to jail for a variety of different offenses like drug possession, stolen vehicles, warrants, hit and run, murder, you name it. We were often asked by law enforcement to share our security surveillance videos with them to aid in the capture of suspected criminals who just happened to stop by our station to buy gas.

One time at our Pacoima gas station, there was an LAPD officer who apparently just went through a very ugly divorce, so he pulled into our station, got out of his car and climbed up a tree on our property. He then drew his gun from its holster and pointed it at different people walking down the block. Other officers were immediately called and came to talk him out of the tree.

There were gang drive-by shootings right in front of that station all the time, and it was actually robbed twice (the only two robberies that we have ever experienced). After each robbery, I would lose a good employee because they never wanted to come back to work after having a gun stuck in their face and their life threatened. I totally understood. Amazingly, I have never had a gun pointed at me in all the years that I have been in this business. It was a very rough neighborhood and I was very happy and relieved when it finally sold in the 1980's.

We have helped the police put many criminals behind bars, sometimes even our own employees! We have had workers steal cash from us, and also steal from our customers by "forgetting" to give them back their credit cards (using them instead to purchase gas and cigarettes for their own personal use). One employee, many years ago, took about $1,000 from different customer's credit cards before we caught him. Credit card fraud is a federal offense, and so I had him arrested for it. I originally hired him based on the recommendations of a friend. I now only trust my own due diligence in researching and doing background checks on prospective employees. Other gas station owners who were not as vigilant as me when hiring the right personal would often lose tens of thousands of dollars before they would discover the theft.

I have come to the conclusion over the years that under the right conditions, most everyone will steal, except for a small percentage of the population. In fact, studies show that 79% of all employees steal from their employers, and is the cause for one out of every three business failures in this country. Actually, 21% will never steal from their employer, 13% will steal from their employer no matter what, and 66% will steal if they can justify it in their minds, or if they see others do so without consequences.

It is very difficult finding the right person to hire. If I ever hired the wrong person, they could have taken me to the cleaners. For example, someone who is desperate or greedy for money is likely to steal. For this reason, I would always try not to hire anyone who was in dire financial straits (desperate) or lived beyond their means (greedy). This is the kind of person who would either steal food to feed their family, or could not make enough money because they were never content with what they already had.

Another reason employees will steal is because they somehow think that their employer owes them something for some injustice committed against them. For this reason, I would always try to not give any employee a reason to think that I am wronging them in any way. I would pay them a fair wage, take them on company sailing trips, and would always treat them with dignity and respect.

The third reason employees will steal is simply because it is easy to do so and there aren't any consequences for the theft. For this reason, I had 19 security cameras installed at the station (most of which were watching the employees). I would also regularly watch the videos of the cashier doing cash register transactions, and I would check for any red flags that would indicate signs of stealing on their shift sheets. I have always fired employees suspected of stealing and have always legally prosecuted any employee theft that I could prove.

Having said all of that, I must explain that over the years we learned how to hire the right employees whose risk of stealing was very, very low. We trusted our employees, but we still watched them for the reasons stated above. As a result, we have not had any of the problems that other gas stations have had with dishonest workers, and we are very grateful for that.

On a happier note, we regularly have movie producers pay us money to shut down the gas station in order for them to shoot a commercial, a movie or a television series. They would pay us about $10,000 which compensated us for the income that we would lose while closed. I was so excited when the producers of the Showtime series, "Weeds," asked me to not only film an episode at our location for the day (and well into the night), but also to play a part in the show (to act as a cashier—uh... that was hard).

Our gas station also had a coffee drive- thru business in the minimart, so during the shooting of the "Weeds" episode, we sold over 100 lattes to the production crew and the actors. The catering trucks served a fantastic breakfast, lunch, dinner and snacks, which we also had access to. It was a lot of fun.

I was telling all my friends to tune into my Hollywood television debut, because I was going to be on "Weeds." However, the episode must have run a little too long, because they had edited out my part. I was so sad and disappointed because my acting scene in the film was cut out and left on the editing room floor. ⌐

Another time, our gas station was honored with the presence of Huell Houser and his "California Gold" television series on public television. He wanted to do a show at our location where he would just walk up to people pumping gas and ask them where they were going and what they were doing in Castaic. It was a very interesting program. He was surprised at how our station had an amazing cross-section of very interesting people from all different walks of life traveling through here.

Chapter 11

Dealing With The Oil Companies

In California, oil companies operate in a way that is very similar to a legal monopoly; let's just call it an oligopoly. An oligopoly is a market form in which a market or industry is dominated by a small number of sellers. A general lack of competition can lead to higher costs for consumers. The reason for this is that the state's gasoline market is essentially closed. The state's strict clean-air rules mandate a specially formulated blend of gasoline that is used nowhere else in the country. Producers in places such as Louisiana or Texas could make it, but there are no pipelines to move it to the West Coast quickly or cheaply.

As a result, virtually all 14.6 billion gallons of gasoline sold in California in 2012 were produced by the nine companies that own the state's refineries. Three of these companies (Chevron, Tesoro and BP) control 54% of the state's refining capacity. Californians basically live on a gasoline island. The control that these oil company-owned refiners have in California is a result of the closed market that the state regulators have created.

Shielded from outside competition, these refiners benefit from keeping the supplies of gasoline tight (reducing the supply of gas made available to the marketplace to keep the price artificially high). Even though California gas consumption has declined in recent years because of high unemployment and increased vehicle fuel efficiency, California's refiners have still been able to keep prices about thirty-five cents per gallon higher than the rest of the country. At the same time, the number of refineries operating in California today has declined from 27 to 14 in the past 30 years.

The lack of competition is also reflected at the retail level. About 85% of California's gas stations sell brand-named fuels such as Mobil, Chevron, Shell, Valero, etc. These are directly or indirectly controlled by these major oil refiners. That leaves only 15% of California's gas stations selling independent (non-brand- named). In other states, like Texas, that number of independents could go as high as 50% which creates more competition. California used to have many more independents back in the 1980s, but due to the consolidation and merging of major oil companies there ended up being fewer oil companies with more money and greater power.

This shift caused a decrease in independent oil companies. As a result, the independents are the first to suffer in a shortage instead of being able to offer additional supplies of cheaper fuel as they had in the past. This fuel used to be purchased on the open market from independently owned refiners that are not owned or controlled by the major oil companies. It's almost as if the major oil companies planned on eliminating the independent refineries because they were threating the major oil company's' control of the marketplace. The independent population is now so small that the major oil companies can control them during times of reduced fuel supply. During times of excess fuel supply, the major companies can still use the independents by selling them unbranded gasoline (brand-named fuel sold at a discount) from the excess supply of their own stations.

Most recently, British Petroleum agreed to sell its refinery (in Carson, California) along with the Arco brand-name to Tesoro. If the transaction is approved by regulators, just two companies - Tesoro and Chevron - will control more than half of the state's gasoline refineries. Some industry experts expect this transaction to lead to even higher gas prices.

It costs as much as fifteen cents a gallon more to refine the state's clean-fuel blend. State fuel excise taxes are also higher in California than in any other state. In addition, lawmakers levied a "temporary" sales tax on gasoline back in the 1980's and we have yet to see this temporary tax go away. This makes California among only seven states that charge sales tax on gasoline. Many experts are predicting the creation of new state laws intended to limit greenhouse gas emissions and encourage alternative fuels. This could force as many as eight of California's refineries to close in the coming years. As the number of refineries in California decreases, the chances of increased disruptive shortages and painful price hikes dramatically increase.

In the financial markets around the world, crude oil future contracts are bought and sold in the same way as corn, wheat, copper, and pork-belly futures. These things are known in financial markets as commodities. Who buys the contracts? Eventually, the contract ownership will end up being bought by companies which really need the commodity to be delivered. But with so much additional demand caused by speculation, the price is usually higher. Recently, more speculators have gotten into the oil futures commodities business. Because of the action of speculators in energy commodities, the farmer and the manufacturer must compete with these speculators to buy fuel, accounting for higher prices.

So, who is to blame for higher gas prices? Oil refiners blame government's strict and costly environmental regulations. They also fault commodity speculators on Wall Street for the instability of gasoline prices. On the other hand, environmentalists usually blame refiners for exploiting and justifying their argument that anti-pollution controls are continually increasing the cost of doing business. No new refineries have been built in decades, despite numerous closures across the nation, especially in California.

It has been an educational experience for me and my family in our dealings with the oil companies during these past sixty-seven years.

The one thing that we have discovered is that the oil companies will ALWAYS do, financially, what is in their best interest. There is no negotiating with them on rent, real estate terms, rebates on fuel purchases and the like.

Their attitude is simply, "Take it or leave it."

The corporate culture has dramatically changed since the 1980's. Deregulation has given corporations a lot more freedom to act without fear of government intervention. As I mentioned before, corporate conscience has been replaced with corporate greed. Capitalism works very well, but only when government does their job in protecting small business and entrepreneurs from anti-competitive behavior.

In my opinion, deregulation has gone too far, giving corporations and industries too much of what they desire; more and more mergers that left fewer and fewer competitors. After their mergers, these giant mega-corporations (who were often in multiple industries) are now the new monopolies that stifle competition and hurt small independent business. Capitalism is getting a bad reputation to the rest of the world as a result. Our regulators (who are supposed to be protecting small business) are nowhere to be found doing their job.

As a result, oil companies have become more arrogant. They have treated their dealers unfairly and have caused many of them to go out of business, simply to satisfy their insatiable appetite for more profit. Even the oil company marketing executives (who we had become friends with over the decades) found themselves becoming the oil companies' mouth piece for implementing more and more unfair policies. These company reps had no choice but to carry out the oil company's unfair policies against the dealer. Policies like demanding a 12% return on investment to calculate rents, when the economy was in the worst economic recession since the Great Depression of the 1930's. Today, no landlords are getting that high of a return on their commercial rents except for the oil industry.

The dealers were not treated like the franchise partners that they are, but instead, as an adversary. Even now, dealers finally have the legal right to purchase from the oil companies the real estate underneath their gas stations. This is a result of state and federal laws that require the oil companies to make bona fide offers to their dealers whenever they sell to any third party. However, most of the oil company's bona fide offers were grossly over-priced; many were over double the fair market value. They also made it almost impossible for a bank to approve any real estate loan for the dealer to buy their gas stations. Our particular oil company stated that they would not be responsible for cleaning up contaminated soil underneath the property (which violates state and federal laws). No other oil company was arrogant enough to insert this stipulation into their dealer's purchase agreement contract.

These dealers finally had no choice but to file a joint lawsuit against their respective oil companies just to be able to buy their gas stations at fair prices and terms. All I can say is shame on the oil companies for treating their dealers so dishonorably and being so ungrateful for the decades of blood, sweat and tears that they provided to the oil industry.

In spite of all this, I am grateful for the previous oil company executive (before the merger) that selected me to become the dealer at my location during the energy crisis of 1979, when it was impossible to even acquire a gas station. That later merger, I believe, destroyed what little soul the original company had. Back then, the oil company actually cared more about their dealer's success than they do today. But now, the future of this business has become very uncertain. Environmental regulations, hybrid and electric cars, solar and alternative power sources, and new technologies promise innovative fuels being made from water, manure, oxygen, corn and other renewable sources. These are the new challenges facing the oil and gasoline industry today.

Increased environmental laws and regulations could be the final nail in the dealer's coffin. The dealer's pockets are not as deep as the oil companies with which to pay for all of those new environmental regulations and equipment that have yet to be legislated. Thank God that I will be old enough to either retire, or die before all this happens. As I always like to say, "I don't know what the future holds, but I know who holds my future." It is my hope that this book has been a source of entertainment for you, and that many of your questions about gas station and oil company practices have been answered. It was fun for me to relive my experiences with you, and I thank you all for allowing me to share. Feel free to e-mail me at Dave@Nassaney.TV with any questions you may have that were not answered in this book.

My website: www.GasolineSecrets.com You may also be interested in reading my previous book that I co-authored last year with my wife, Charlene, about our life-journey together,

Acknowledgements

My very special thanks go to Charlene Nassaney, Eddie Neate, Marilee Thurman, Maryalice Pierce, and Fritzie Nagel for their help and input in the early editing of this manuscript. I especially wish to thank Kris Ornelas for sharing his special talents and precious time in helping me polish the final edits of this book. Also, to all the people (you know who you are) who helped me with my first book. Because of your efforts, writing this book was so much easier. I also want to thank every employee who ever worked for me since 1976 that stomached all of the rest room challenges. Through it all, you were able to learn graciousness, patience and professionalism, and I believe that you are a better person as a result.

A very special thank you goes to my two former managers, Jack Terrana and Okal (J.R.) Searcy III. Jack worked for me the first fifteen years and J.R. worked the second. They were both very faithful and loyal team members and helped provide a pleasant buying experience to all of our customers. May you both continue to have

Other Books By Dave Nassaney

"One Arm One Leg 100 Words,
Overcoming Unbelievable
Hardships"

"It's Your Life Too, How to Survive
& Thrive as a Caregiver"

Dave's Newest #1 Best-Seller

"Secrets From the Hammock Uncommon
Wisdom for Uncommon Times"

...On sale wherever books are sold

Also, check out our websites,

www.DaveNassaney.com
www.CaregiverDave.com
www.GasolineSecrets.com
www.GasolineExpert.com

My present location since 1979
Coffee Stop Drive-Thru & Mobil
31785 The Old Rd. Castaic, CA. 91384

Made in the USA
Monee, IL
25 June 2022

98600274R00056